On the Wings of Sound

Images of Hope

Tom Motika

On the Wings of Sound
Copyright © 2024 by Tom Motika
All Rights Reserved

No part of this book may be reproduced or transmitted in any form or by any means, electronic or mechanical, including photocopying, recording, or by any information storage and retrieval system without the written permission of the author, except where permitted by law.

For Pat.

Acknowledgments

Thanks to my wife Pat and sons Tim and Jim for supporting my poetry in so many ways. Another thanks to my grandson Aneirin for the cover idea.

Thanks also to two wonderful English professors, Father Gerber from the University of Notre Dame and Doug Burger from the University of Colorado.

Table of Contents

Poetic Journey 1

    This Will Just Take a Few Seconds 3

    On the Way to the Bus Stop 5

    What Sweet Light 6

    The Temple Of Tears 7

    Inspiration 8

    The Subway 9

    Hospital Diary 11

    Beyond the Stars 13

    For Pat 14

    Old Seth 15

    A Proposed Merger That Is Serious Business 17

    The Glory of War 19

    And I Was Born 20

    Shakespeare's Great 21

    Darker Moments Have I Known 22

    Prometheus Bound 23

    The Quiet Moment 24

    Knowledge and the Dreamer 25

Images 27

Stones of Fire 29

Pools of Visitation 30

The Sky 31

The Scarab 33

The Moon 34

Mother Goose and I 35

Songs 37

Windowpane 39

My Mind Was in the Gutter 40

The River of Smiles 41

Every Day 43

Bring Me a Sad Note 44

I'm Going to Sing 45

Seven-Foot Cherries 46

Spiritual Poems 47

Now I Lay Me Down to Sleep 49

Lay Down the Lion 50

The Real Contract 51

A Blind Man Talks to God 52

Humor 53
   A Singer of Note 55
   I Know a Little Rabbit 56
   The Little Brown Mouse 57
   His Name Was So Short 58
   I Lose a Foot 59
   I'm Down 60
   Seven Card Stud 61
   The Land of Quandary 62
   The Knight's Horse 63
   The Enchanted Forest 64
   There Was a Rich Dentist 65
   The Danger of a Hyphenated Name 66
   There Was an Old Man 67
   An Ignorant Slob 68
   Doodles Day 69
About the Author 71

Poetic Journey

This Will Just Take a Few Seconds....

After all, what can happen in a single second?

- The winning basket with the ball thrown from across the court.

- The game's final touchdown with the football gliding effortlessly into the receiver's hands.

- An Olympic World Record where achievement is measured in hundredths of a second.

A second can be the difference between life and death: the time to reach out and grab someone about to fall; the time to leap out of the way of a speeding car; the time to decide not to do the idiot thing that will get you killed. A second is enough time to discover the love of your life. A second is forever.

Every day you receive 86,400 forevers.

You can't hold on to them. You can only watch them go or you can give them away.

Given to someone else, they become part of that person, part of their 86,400 forevers every day.

Given with love, they last. We see them in a building, a painting, a piece of furniture, a photograph. We hear them in a song, in a movie, in the words of someone we love. We live them over and over again.

A second is forever. You have 86,400 to give away today.

On the Way to the Bus Stop

Who would blame the summer birds
For staying on till spring?
The sun has poured a morning
That makes January sing.

The honey liquor of his light
Has drenched the eastern plains.
It washes every window
And seeps into the drains.

This summer brew that fills my eyes
Makes me stagger like a fool.
It's washed the windows of my soul
And left it shining like a jewel.

What Sweet Light

What sweet light bends over the world
And kisses the cold, wet ground?

Who will touch these cold, wet eyes
When they are full of tears and death?

Who will miss them,
Who will kiss them,
Who will feel my parting breath?

What sweet light bends over the world
And kisses the cold, wet ground –
Kisses me.

The Temple Of Tears

Beneath the waters of my soul
I keep a simple shrine.
All the tears that went unwept
Are bottled there like wine.

I cannot break the temple door.
I have no temple key,
But in my dreams, I enter –
And drink my misery.

Once I did cry out to God,
"What use is unspent grief?"
"Through tears thou see
Thy brother's need
And help his unbelief."

Inspiration

I wanted to write a poem
Of images and tenderness,
A poem like the ones
Of Gabriela Mistral.

I wrote about the mountains
That overlook my city.
My images weighed nothing.
Her words are like stones.

I gazed at the jagged mountains
That look down upon the city,
Their faces battered by the rain,
Their shoulders bruised by the wind.

Suffering broke her words
Into images of tenderness.
Love wrote her soul
Into poems of truth.

The Subway

The way to the world lies
underground in the subway of the heart. It runs
daily on rubber tires (as the ones in Paris) with
the two headlights gleaming as the carriages
round the bend for the station.

Quietly, though new, it squeals a little and stops.

"Enter," she says.

"Why must I always take the first class carriages,
the yellow ones?"

"This is the journey to your own soul
and only first class is good enough for that kind of travel."

The train lurches and makes way
with a grinding whine from the tires,
hurtling madly along the track.

"The agony of First Class",
I say, reaching for the solidness of the bottom of the wooden seat,
"Is that you travel alone."

"Naturally," she says with a smile.

Hospital Diary

They took the cancer in my sleep.
I did not see it go.
I woke; my wife was standing near.
It was she who told me so.

A plastic bag above the bed,
With a tube down in my vein,
Brings the food and all my drink
And even stops the pain.

Three more bags and three more tubes
All drain a part of me.
The nurses come and change the bags;
It works efficiently.

I brought eight books; they're in a drawer.
I barely watch TV.
My wife, my son, and friends all come.
I cannot scream, "Why me?"

It's two more days at 2:00 a.m.
The clock hands will not move.
I'm cold, so cold, my breath so slow –

I pray, "Jesus, send your love."
When a snap of the blinds fills the room with sun,
I wake to see it's so.
Who took my fever and my rage?
I did not feel them go.

The doctors stream in with the sun,
Their eyes filled with concern.
Gone is the nurse who watched me breathe
And phoned each one in turn.

My wife brings me a magazine
And helps me wheel the stand
That holds my bags and tubes. We walk
Together, hand in hand.

Bob left a puzzle; Connie, some toys.
Most just leave what they say –
Like Jim, who said how his failing heart
Let him see each precious day.

Each brings a treasure for me to keep;
I watch them come and go.
When they took the cancer in my sleep,
I never dreamed it so.

Beyond the Stars

When all the streaming stars
Fall into oblivion, who cares?
Who made the universe can
Make the universe again.

We stand in awe
Admiring ourselves,
Basking in our inventions
Of god [always in lower case],
Recalling today's news,
Noting the flicker of the past,
Recounting our gains and losses.

Heaven is beyond the stars.

For Pat

Shall I compare thee
To a summer's day?
Or the stars, the moon,
Or some sweet tune
Or lover's lay?

Nay, I shall compare
Them all to thee.

Old Seth

Old Seth, sittin' by the fire,
Coat crumpled round his shoulders,
Sweater showin' through his sleeve.
Sittin' there, he don't care
Whether you stay or leave.

Hummin' to himself,
Thinkin' to himself,
Drinkin' for everyone.

Bought him a cup of coffee
For a little change of pace.
Came back to the table
Smiles run through his face,

With his hair like long grass,
And his beard like long grass,
And his eyes like two kids playin',
Like two children, in the long grass.

Old Seth sittin' by a wall,
Old man sittin' neath a tree
Do old fires come back again?
'Cause old faces come back to me.

Seth sittin' there in his old, fat coat
Tuckin' his scarf around his throat.
Do he come back again?
No, he just don't go 'way.

A Proposed Merger That Is Serious Business

Every day and every night
I come back to the room
Like a castle on a hilltop
Or an undiscovered tomb.

And I'm prepared to make delivery
Of some confidential papers
That set the real estate in your hands,
To carry the transaction
With no need for a down payment,
Just a verbal understanding,
And one who understands,
And one who understands.

Every morning, and every evening
I come back and I'm alone.
With the furniture and bric-a-brac,
You'd hardly call it home.

So I'm prepared for an agreement
That allows a choice investment
Far beyond your dreams,
Yet in keeping with your means.
It will grow as equity in your hands,
In your hands.
I'm prepared this very moment
To consider such a merger
With your likely talents
In a partnership guaranteed unconditionally.
Well, it means a lot to me.
Well, it means a lot to me.

This mornin' and this evening
I found the company lacking
And my mind and soul were grieving
'Cause I'm more than company backing.

So I'm prepared to consider
A venture upon the open market,
A sale and purchase of some shares – to spare.
The bid for our security
Is the corporate bond between us.
It's the fact that we can care.
It's the fact that we can care.

The Glory of War

A child plays upon a hill
With planes and ships at his command.
He moves his troops with speed and skill
Surrounded by the desert sand.
The Glory of War.

But when he raises up his head,
His open lids show shattered eyes,
Devoid of all but hopeless dread.
The desert echoes with his cries,
"I am no more!"

"A beast has entered into man
That drinks his will and seeks control.
Life and death are but its plan
To drain away the human soul.
Fear it, therefore!"

And I Was Born

And I was born,
The ground to kiss my every step,
The air to catch my breath
The earth to clutch a lover's love,
And time to hold my death.

Shakespeare's Great

I mean, sir, I think we understand,
Lear is great and timeless (for those
Who can appreciate his age) –
But did his shouting get anything done?
I know tragedy isn't supposed to do anything,
But, well then, you see, isn't it all very trite?
I mean who can feel for a a fellow who
Runs around England,
Screaming at storm clouds,
Dirty, disheveled, betwigged,
Simply because of poor planning?
I mean I realize it's tragedy and
Good for all that emotional release
(Reduces tension, helps clear out the cobwebs)
But what good is Lear?
I mean – you know – the daughters die,
And everybody else that we got to know
And admire dies, or just about bores us
To death with that crowning – God, what nobility!
But I agree Shakespeare was the greatest
And as they say, a thing worth doing is worth doing
well.

Darker Moments Have I Known

There were darker moments.
When evening leaves the shadows of the day
And day itself becomes shadow,
When softly stealing diseases of the mind
Pass for the best intent,
And all the world dissolves
In something less than bliss.
Darker moments have I known.

Prometheus Bound

A spectral dot between the clouds
Circles aloft on sun-tipped wings.
I gaze upon it fixedly
And feel the chafe of iron rings.
At my feet a cricket sings.

The air is shattered by a piercing scream
As downward drops the distant form,
Slicing the wind on razor wings
It sweeps the plains, looming like a storm
Over my body, sentient and warm.

The eagle lands and folds its wings,
Then rips my side with a single claw.
It plunges in its hungry beak
And feeds, once more devouring both raw
Flesh and my soul's fire in its craw.

Sated, the bird stands erect and preens.
Regarding my chains with a glittering eye,
It shakes and spreads its golden wings,
Then springs, soaring into the sky.
To man, its form is majesty.

The Quiet Moment

The quiet moment is stricken with the frenzy of its passing.
Hands, busy hands, bring the hour to its
Conclusion of collusion with the unseen.
Quiet hands, noiseless, tremble in expectation.
Busy hands, busy minds bury what their system finds
In the catacombs and rinds of expected answers.

Knowledge and the Dreamer

Darkness grows on winter wings.
Heaven knows,
And counts the dear, mysterious things
That even darkness brings.

All time is darkness
To this man's eye.
With glass on glass
He probes the morning sky
Reflecting and refracting
 An inquisitive solar eye.

Sleep corrupts the vision on the lens
As evening sings and makes amends
With magnitudes of suns in darkness.

Darkness grows on winter wings.
Heaven knows,
And counts the dear, mysterious things
That even darkness brings.

Images

Stones of Fire

Stones of fire
Do not speak
And when touched
They even break.

Stones of heat
Whose glowing core is love--
I touched them once.

Pools of Visitation

Pools of visitation
Pools beyond the darkling eye of morn
Pools of invitation

The fishes do not murmur
In the pools of visitation
The starbird does not thunder,
Does not beat his fiery wings
In the darkling morn.

The pools are pools of silence
The reeds wander in the waters
Touched by the dark breath
Of the deep spring
Rising, Feeding
The pools of silence.
The reeds do not touch
Beneath the waters of visitation.

The Sky

Morning

The sun, like some steady spark
Searing the purple gloom,
Leaves the east aflame.
And the clouds do blush the more,
Discovered in sleepy caress
With the earth.

Spring Morning

In spring, the morning sun lingers,
Watching the stars as they fade in the dawn,
Then touches the dewdrops with playful fingers,
Making a galaxy on the lawn.

Sky

When in the leafy stillness,
Broken only by a footstep,
I could stand and measure out
The sky in scattered plots of blue and white --
And call it mine.
God, who's rich now?

Another Sky

You say sky. No, it is more. An unearthly
Sea that winds around the world, and
Drops its currents for birds, and kites,
And dust. Great galleons of clouds
Billow to catch the wind and slip across
The face of the universe. Who cannot say
It is an ocean, when those black
And ominous ships rain the earth with fire.

The Scarab

A scarab born of earthly romance
Is enough to tell the secrets of our days.
Mesmerized upon a tomb
The pharaoh keeps his court elsewhere now.
A scarab brings the news in dust.

The Moon

"The stars, "I cry, "the stars,
They carry out to sea.
But the moon, the moon," I said
"Remembers only me."

Wandering scarred face,
Circled and half circled,
Setting up slow shop
In a singsong, nighttime escapade.

I throw up my hands at your fickle ways.
One look back, before you slip over the mountain.

Wink.

Mother Goose and I

Silver apples, red, red roses
Lie upon the road.
Take them up and fill your cup.
They lighten any load.

Peek-a-boo grass,
Push the snow back.
Make way for
The crocus and the lilac.

Ten dollars up,
Ten cents down
Bakes you a cake
And buys you a crown.

Songs

Windowpane

Windowpane, isn't going anywhere
Inside, outside, in-between.
Window glass, just for looking out of,
Can't be touched, or smudged, or seen.

Refrain
Around the world people are there
At their windows everywhere
Finding a world in a windowpane.

Morning sun, enough to wake the living up,
Slip past my window and call on me.
Evening shade, wash my window of the day.
Bring my friend who looks like me.

My Mind Was in the Gutter

I see the whirling brown water
Cascading in streams
Catching in snatches
The falling sunbeams
In a falls from a grate
That only serves to drain away the rain.

Refrain
Isn't it wonderful,
Isn't it wonderful,
Just to find a place
With a beautiful gutterful.

I hear the rushing brown water
In railway time
Leaving and sweeping
Bacterial grime
Through a network of cracks
That serve micro-miles of stony grooves.

The River of Smiles

They laid Papa in a stone cold grave.
Preacher knew his soul was hard to save.
Too little money so what did he give?
And everybody knew just where he lived,
But nobody there saw Papa wave.

He's sailin', he's sailin' on the River of Light.
His failings have sailed out of sight.
With the sun on the river
And the water washin' the side,
His hand's on the tiller
He rides, he rides
The River of Light
The River of Smiles.

Rain keeps pourin' on the funeral tent.
They shoveled down the dirt when the preacher went.
Y' know, Papa pushed a broom while he was alive,
Hung around bars and cheap little dives
And everybody knew he didn't repent.

I'm here with you on the River of Light
When the world don't care for you
They build your casket right.
With the wind at my shoulders
And the sun on my face,
If you ain't got nobody
You always got a place
On the River of Light,
The River of Smiles.

Papa, he helps those dyin' around,
But first gets the poor and the broken down,
Cause they ain't got no else to care.
They don't take nothin', cause there's nothin' to spare
And they don't mind being found.

I come for you on the River of Light.
When the world ain't there for you
And you lose your sight.
With the sun round my shoulder
And a star over our heads
I'll lift you in my hands
And take you from your bed
To the River of Light
The River of Smiles.

Every Day

Every day it seems a little brighter
As the sun climbs into my room
Every hour it grows a little higher and lighter
Until it reaches noon.

Refrain
The time is ripe
The day is fat upon the land
And it's all our lives
To catch the apples of the sun
And set their seeds to earth.

Every hour I feel a little stronger
As the light grows brighter in my eyes.
Every minute seems ever so much longer and finer
As I put by my disguise.

Bring Me a Sad Note

Bring me a sad note
I'll bring you the day.
Bring me your sorrow
And I'll bring you away,
Bring you away, lass
I'll bring you away.

Words are like water
Glass is the sea
Bring me a bottle
And my lass to me,
And my lass to me, love
And my lass to me.

Oceans of roses
Sleep till the morn
Petals unopened
Are you still warm?
Are you still warm, lass
Are you still warm?

I'm Going to Sing

I'm going to sing
I'm going to laugh
I'm going away
Just to come back.

I'm going to lay you
Down beside me
I'm going to play it
The way I see.
I'm going to leave,
Leave you smiling
I'm going to bring you home.

I'm going to laugh
I'm going to sing
I'm going to bring you
A pretty thing.

Seven-Foot Cherries

Seven-foot cherries for the hunger-starved,
A little hug for the friendless,
But who takes care of the wonder-starved
Whose appetite is endless.

Refrain
Say I'm hungry, say I'm bored.
What's the reason anymore?
Say I'm out of style.
Call me bastard.
Call me child.
Nothing holds me like before.

Thunderstorms for thirsty men,
A nickel for the poor,
Death just gets his curtsy in,
Is there more? Is there more?

Spiritual Poems

Now I Lay Me Down to Sleep

Now I lay me down to sleep
Gentle rest my brothers
Hear our laughter
Hear us weep
Gentle keep us all

And if I miss the morning sun
Gentle let you take my hand
O Lord, bless everyone
Gentle joy for all.

Lay Down the Lion

They lay down weary
To waken weary
In every home.
Each bears a fate
To face all alone.
Each sees friends
Dying beside them.
Gentle I beckon them all.

Refrain
Lay down the lion
Lay down the lamb
And lay down the child
In the peaceable kingdom for all

They do go gentle
And lay down gentle
Beside the lamb.
Each one a child,
They come as they can.
Each child is mine
Who lay down beside me
Gentle I care for them all.

The Real Contract

I stand and see Your loving grace
In all I do. Is it enough?
Why would I think to take Your place?
The lust to control is drug-like stuff.

Lord, let it all be Yours – again.
How many times I give it all
To You, yet still it is mine. Then
The taste of glory is the taste of gall.

I hold here this simple pen and vow
That I shall no more take in hand
The hour and the end. No matter how
It comes, I see Your grace and command.

Let this be said. Let it be done.
That You and I may be as one.

A Blind Man Talks to God

Man: Wilt thou give me grace and praise?

God: Is this how thou wouldst spend thy days,
With grace and praise?

Man: Wilt thou let me do thy will?

God: When thou hast no more tears to spill,
Wilt thou do my will?

Man: Wilt thou give and let me love?

God: Who art thou thinking of,
To give and let thy love?

Man: What shall I say?

God: That thou dost pray
My will be done.
Open up thy star-filled eyes,
Put away thy mournful cries,
And be my son.

Humor

A Singer of Note

A singer of note
Caught a fly in his throat
Which to him was was rather phenomenal.
Said the Fly
"Me, O my,
Though I'm now high and dry
My future looks really abdominal."

But the singer knew slang
Which he ponderously sang,
And using it like a gargle,
Tossed the Fly in the sky
Who said, "Me, O my,
I've been saved by a largo of argot."

I Know a Little Rabbit

I know a little rabbit
That has the silly habit
Of being just a rabbit
And not a dog or cat.

He doesn't find it funny
If you call him bunny.
They're just too cute and sunny,
And sometimes stuffed at that.

The Little Brown Mouse

There's a little brown mouse
Hiding under the stair.
No one in the house,
Not even the cat, knows he's there.

He sneaks out at night
To look for some cheese.
He doesn't say thank you or please.

There's a little brown mouse
Washing his whiskers and face
He's had a small dinner
And now for a nap just in case--

He sneaks out tonight
To meet Miss Mousette.
They'll need a new home soon I bet.

There's a new little hole
Opening under the stair.
It's just by the coal,
But shhh, don't breathe a word who is there.

His Name Was So Short

His name was so short
That when said with a snort
It left him a pile of money.

There was gold in a chest
And a check for the rest,
And on Easter a chocolate bunny.

I Lose a Foot

I lose a foot,
I lose my toes,
When I cross my eyes
In front of my nose.

I'm Down

I'm down,
I can't get up no more.
My chin's been restin' on my shoes,
I got nothin' else to lose
'Cause I'm always standing under the floor.

Seven Card Stud

Seven card stud's a handy game.
I win it all the time.
The hole card knows
I've lost my clothes
And, "Could you spare a dime?"

Note: In stud poker the 'hole card' is the one not showing. The other six cards are face up.

The Land of Quandary

A lugubrious moose of dubious use
Was wandering through a Quandary.
Though the mire was high,
He kept himself dry
By wrapping his feet in his laundry.

Now I know there are some who become rather dumb
When they fall in the state of quandary.
You don't just drive by.
You must drop from the sky
And the sand where you land is the boundary

All its natives have flunked
For their heads are preshrunk in a land too far to be walked to.
So they sit in the shade
And sip lemonade
Where the flowers don't fade it they're talked to.

The Knight's Horse

His horse was white, as was naturally right
Of a study as brown as a berry
And he shone so at night
That the knight in the light
Couldn't sleep much, no not very.

The Enchanted Forest

A forest was near
And t'was highly unclear
If the trees were peaches or prunes.
For the day was ending
And the trees were mending
Their leaves by the light of the moon.

There Was a Rich Dentist

There was a rich dentist from Lief
Who kept all his gold in his teeth.
While he slept, they got stolen.
False teeth for a false one.
And the dentist couldn't speak for his grief.

The Danger of a Hyphenated Name

There was a young man named Miller
Whose name was really a filler.
He was Polish and Sioux.
What could his wife do?
His real name would kill her.

There Was an Old Man

There was an old man who wrote Greek,
And some there said he could speak
It and would,
That is, if he could.
But the Greek got stuck in his cheek.

An Ignorant Slob

An ignorant slob
With a head like a blob
Peeked through a door
And was mistook for the knob.

Doodles Day

It's Doodles Day. It's Doodles Day
What can I say
Hurray, Hurray
It's Doodles Day. It's Doodles Day

There's Noodles Day
And Oodles Day
And even
Oodles of Noodles Day
That's not a bit like Doodles Day

There's Toodles Day
And Boodles Day
And even
Boodles of Toodles Day
Where everyone says Goodbye
On Doodles Day
We all say Hi!

On Doodles Day
We come to laugh
We come to play.
So much to do for me and you.
A day in every color too.
Hurray! Hurray!
It's Doodles Day!

About the Author

Tom Motika grew up in Denver and graduated from the University of Colorado. He majored in Theater because he wanted to see words in action and stories come to life. He read constantly, searching for inspiration by reading poems and stories from every continent. As he began writing poems, he found his way into computers with an entry-level job. Technology was another continent of language. While writing poetry, he spent over 30 years in his career as programmer, analyst, and project manager. Better lines of code and technical explanations were all about learning to write clear, simple words for poetry.

www.ingramcontent.com/pod-product-compliance
Lightning Source LLC
Chambersburg PA
CBHW041149110526
44590CB00027B/4169